NATIONAL GEOGRAPHIC

Making Music

Elaine Morris

Do you know how the sound of music is made?

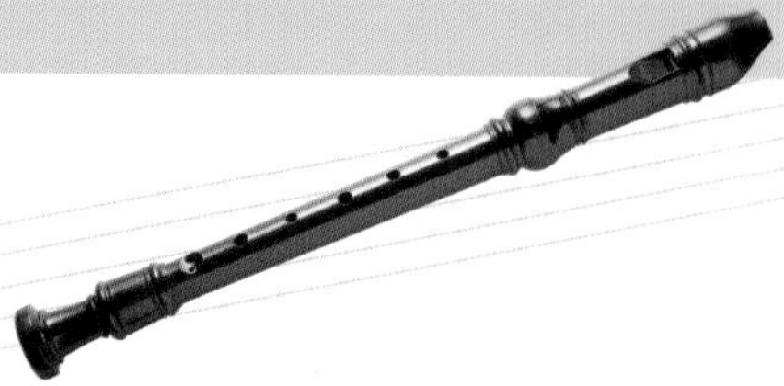

All the musical instruments vibrate, or move back and forth quickly. When an instrument vibrates, it makes sounds that travel through the air. We hear music when these sounds reach our ears.

We can use a drum to make music. A drum has a thin cover called a drumhead. We use sticks to beat the drumhead. Beating the drumhead makes it vibrate.

We can use a guitar to make music. A guitar has strings. We use our hands to pluck the guitar strings. Plucking the strings makes them vibrate.

We can use a tambourine to make music. A tambourine has many small metal disks. We use our hands to shake the tambourine. Shaking the tambourine makes the metal disks vibrate.

We can use a recorder to make music. A recorder has an opening with a small plug inside. We use our mouth to blow into the opening. Blowing into the opening makes the plug vibrate.

What other instruments can we use to make music?